As If To Sing

for Joe, Jack and Ioan

As If To Sing

Paul Henry

SEREN

Seren is the book imprint of
Poetry Wales Press Ltd.
Suite 6, 4 Derwen Road, Bridgend, Wales, CF31 1LH
www.serenbooks.com
facebook.com/SerenBooks
twitter@SerenBooks

The right of Paul Henry to be identified as
the author of this work has been asserted in accordance
with the Copyright, Designs and Patents Act, 1988.

© Paul Henry 2022

ISBN: 9781781726600
Ebook: 9781781726617

A CIP record for this title is available from the British Library.

The publisher acknowledges the financial assistance of the Books Council of Wales.

Cover artwork: 'Angel yw Fy Nghariad' by Anthony Goble

Printed in Bembo by Severn, Gloucester.

Contents

I
As if to Sing

Tributary

I heard a woman's grief in clear water,
a small chamber under a stone
where a tin cup was left, for walkers –
a public grief turned private,
a grief unconscious of its song.
I knelt where her words had burrowed
back inside the hill, her grief to my lips,
her sorrow to my ear. I might have prayed.

The tracery of years, down to the lake.
Some nights I return, to lift the stone,
thinking it's her voice I hear.
The cup is still there.
Moonlight pours into the spring,
her grief to my lips, her sorrow to my ear.

The Glass Door

You knock on the brittle pane,
peering in through your fringe,
a green light through pines.

You knock on the brittle pane.
It is late but I let you in –
your bare feet leaking sand,
your beach-bag full of songs.

And the door stutters open
on a hinge where glass and air
are one element and neither
breaks the other.

              I let you in
to a dusty study, forgetting
to rest my palm against yours
on the pane

          like this, aligned
so the lifelines seal each other.

Cave Songs

Cat, you've caught me inland
sending you this faint light
from Gounod's old torch.

I am inside the limestone cave
where a white fish survived
on darkness for centuries.

See how the beam's baton
moves about the silence
between us, the darkness

how it picks out this wall
in tears, these crotchets
hanging by their feet.

I send you this andante light,
this echo of the sun
because you know the tune

it is trying to conduct
and, Cat, you understand
this might be enough

to hold time in its rock pool.

*

My ghost stood beside me
on stage last night.
He sang a song for you

Cat, a better one
than I tried to write
and with a voice so sad

a flock of cellos settled
on the saltmarsh
and remembered us

to the sea's applause.

★

So I am back inland,
in this hill's dark cell,
sending you this beam

the sleeping bats ignore.
Tell me, was it *Ave Maria*
our mothers preferred?

Their voices find me here.

Fainter still…
I shall have to find an exit.
Cat?

Don't close your eyes, yet.
There is still a little light.
I forget where we came in.

★

I crawl back through water,
decades, to an inlet
where the stone cleaves

into rooms we cannot enter,
rooms we cannot leave –

a school's empty corridor
where you wait forever,
your face in your sleeve.

★

On I go, same moves
across playing fields, stages,
churches where they still believe

in rooms we cannot enter,
rooms we cannot leave.

Laughter now, blue altitudes,
a biplane trailing summers
through clouds that weave

rooms we cannot enter,
rooms we cannot leave.

Through clinics, hotels, prisons,
offices … 'Who shredded
the years' ordered sheaves?'

The rooms we cannot enter,
the rooms we cannot leave.

★

Cat, I am lost, are you?
We are not where we
started out, this maize

echoes on for miles
under the old tramway.
I think it ends at the sea

in Aber, with songs
our mothers sang,

with all the love they gave
and all that they received.

★

... nunc e - t in ho - -   ra,
in ho - - ra- mo - rti-s no- strae ...

I send you this torchsong
Cat, its echo of the sun,

snake through its minims
towards your dusky room.

This must be the way ...

Perhaps they are searching
somewhere above,
falling silent when they

hear the ghost choir,
the tired quarrymen
who autographed this stone.

The water is rising.

Cat, hear me shivering.
And keep this song, its light.

I forget where we came in.

Songs that Bring the Sea to Her Eyes

Press your ear to the white door

which sweeps the Godwin tiles
as we enter.

          Eurydice
warms her hands
on a candle's flame

drifts between two pianos,
an upright and a grand,

dines on lava bread and wine.

Tut-tut says the metronome,
wagging its chapel's finger.

Her voice is a woman's now.
It floods the cavernous hall.

The snake inside the Steinway
lifts his head to hear

O mio babbino caro,
Un bel dì vedremo ...

songs that bring the sea
to her eyes

         Piangerò ...
Vissi d'arte ...

         lifts his head
then sweeps across the tiles
to kiss her feet.

         Tut-tut
says the metronome.

Tauseef Akhtar's Harmonium

Often it disappears – from hotels,
harbours, airport carousels ...
but always it comes back to him.

Trusting in the umbilical dance
of instrument and player
he stays calm in its absence.

Amongst the cosmic flotsam
orbiting Earth this minute
There! Tauseef's harmonium.

On the sea bed, flexing its gills
for ghazal-hungry shoals
Listen! Tauseef's harmonium ...

sometimes for years until,
missing his voice on the air,
it plunges through the atmosphere

or, surfacing back to the light,
steals in on the tide's concertina
to appear at Tauseef's paddling feet –

a child's shadow through frosted glass
after all hope has been lost.

As if to Sing

'… never more beautiful than here under the guns' noise.'
Ivor Gurney – *First Time In*

Their glassy dreams lined the front
and sometimes caught the sun,
the Welsh boys, mouths open
as if to sing.

Last night, for safe-keeping,
they packed their hearts
into a song.

So when only one in four parts
of their harmony
returned, for roll call,
the song still held them all.

Dust o'clock

'Midnight. Midnight. Midnight. Midnight.
Hark at the hands of the clock.'
                    Vernon Watkins – *Ballad of the Mari Lwyd*

New Year's Eve. No horse's head
would make it up this lane.
Answering church bells in the dark
a clock that hasn't talked for years,
on the floor, beside a wicker bin –
a 1930's mantelpiece clock
pronounced dead by John the Clock
about eight-to-twelve ago –
wheezes, then chimes, picks up
if you please, its monologue
at the line it believes it forgot
a second before.

                    I'm back   I'm back
I'm back...   it tocks.
I never left and nor did you.
You're still a suited, married man –
'sinner and saint, sinner and saint ...'
who could not leave his wife and sons.
Your father's not in Hell
but cannot get 'The News at Ten'
however many times he points
his dentures at the screen ...

I rise and kick it hard, the clock
into the Christmas tree, a shower
of needles, seconds plucked.
Its pendulum is shocked
but still it talks.

                    Who is it sings
outside, in the lane?

'Sinner and saint,
sinner and saint …' – workhouse ghosts
on colts, stallions, fillies, mares …
up from the Union canal bridge,
hungry since the first star
knocked on a dark door.

I pick up the cat, check the locks,
cover my clock with an old sack,
cover my ears from the knock-knock-
knock of a horse's head at the door.

I'm back   I'm back   I'm back …
sings the devil in his sack

until his ticking chatter fails
and the bells in the valley hold their tongues
and the ghostly snow horses thaw
and the mice bed down in the walls.

This train has left the city ...

This train has left the city
approximately ten years late.

You sway and stare at the glitter
thinning out into fields,
a Hopper model darkness frames,
your hair tied back, your dress
still thinking it's summer.

We share a cup's hand-warmer.
Here comes a tunnel, a pause
where I cannot hear clearly
the song that nests in your head.
I used to know it by heart.

It's our station already.
Drink up. We were never here.

Somniloquy

Speak into my good ear.
The house is bubble-wrapped
with rain. It's late.

To better hear your voice
through this worn out device
I lean in closer to the page.

To better hear the sleep talk
tangled in its sheets
I lean in closer to your lips.

Speak into my good ear.
The crackle of dark matter
on its way to this room

clears at last, to better hear
your dream ask, *Is it you?*
Where have you been?

Red Moped, Powys

i Twm Morys

There are no speed-limits in dreams.
Village boys in the seventies
we shared its rust.

              Touch the frame.
A brittle parchment falls apart.

The lane's tongue snaked either side
of the Dyke.

            No one was sure
which curly head had swept by.
There are no speed-limits in dreams.

And which of us wrote it off
on wet leaves matters less today
than our going halves on repairs

or that each kept a wheel, for a harp.

Red Phone Box, Powys

Dripping lantern on the verge,
a villager's St Paul's.
Who will clear the grime
and briars from your dome,
the whispers from your walls?

Behind your clouded panes
the dead relight their cigarettes –

a dazed aunt informs the police
Hess has landed,

                    Picker Puw's
sermon makes us wait,

a teenager scratches a heart
and then a prick …

Frayed wick of a mouthpiece,
your glow lit our dreams, your bell
unanswered, deep inside the night,
outrang the pub, the shop, the school …

Burn on, old flame, sheltering now,
at 4am, the paper van's bale.

Avec merci

Inside the copse on the roundabout
she kneels where he lies,
as if to kiss a child good night.

Now lifting his cracked visor
she whispers *Revenir*.
And he tries to come back

but can only dream here –
his blood-soaked destrier
on its side, his torn hauberk –

under her wild wild eyes,
inside the copse of her hair.

Paean for a Cliff Railway Driver

i.m. Ted Pugh

The waves pack down at the sea wall and push.
The town slides back a few decades, digs in
and the wall holds true.

                The student hall's
gallery can't see Llŷr, rising
out of the bay on creaking wings

to start the first ride, pendulous phoenix
up the perilous cliff-face path.
Who will sculpt him?

                The funicular sea
pulls the prom from under us, our dreams.

Llŷr ascends, cursing his leg on the slope
and the morning turns blue at the top.

The waves pack down, tired veterans now.
Students disappear from their frames.
Llŷr watches over the town

                      from his nest,
tilts his driver's cap, unscrews his flask,
raises a cup to Victory and the pier.

He knows the precarious balance of the tides,
keeps his crutches near.

                The twin carriages
rise and fall on their cable

                    pass in the middle,
the town's dead and the town's living.

The sun lays its track to the horizon.
New waves whisper old lies to the shore.
Llŷr's passengers queue.

                          The sea wall
breathes easily, holds true.

Admira and Boško

Crossing a bridge between two lives
I pass your ghosts, still lying here
in each other's arms, in a cast
no Michelangelo comes near.

Forgive this vulturous heart,
a stranger's second-hand grief.
The world rushes on without you
but must not forget your love.

Under its broken wing
the blood-red rivers sing.

Last Move

They swapped a promenade for this lane,
my parents, who cling to each other
for ballast, against an arctic wind.
What madness brought them here,
walking their unsettled souls?
She'll twist an ankle in those heels.
He doesn't know a robin from a hawk,
an approaching son from a stranger.

It is too cold to stop and talk.
Their mournful steps leave no prints.
My mother smiles at my greying hair,
half-raises a gloved hand.
Songs hibernate inside her.
We may not pass like this again.

Nightlines

At once moving and still, the river's trick.

The Fox's chef pays. Breaking-strains are high.
Our fathers' shadows on the bark. Look away.

Sometimes a line disappears, a fish slips its puppeteer
or escapes with a hook in its gill.

                              Trout, eels, salmon …
go into the deep sack. Look away.

                              Our village
swells at the bottom of its well.

                              And on our backs
are stitched the pelts of rabbits. We don't know why.

Our mothers' shadows on the bark, our lineage,
our right to be forgotten.

                              World, turn your blind eye.
The moon is enough to thread a new line by.

Lapping over our tracks, the owl's anonymous cry.

Sleuth

Sometimes the spirit of a man or woman
you had once loved and craved
steps out of a tree, an underground station,
a crowded shop window ... A trick of the sun
has brought them back, plays with their age.
(The *Columbo* raincoat gives it away).
They left your village or town before time,
or you left theirs.

                    Either way, you survived,
were young enough to cry and move on,
cry and move on, and soon it will fade,
this ghost of pain, following close behind
along the quiet lane, the city embankment ...
their steps a beat out but still in chime
almost, with yours, as you break into a run.

Waiting for Steph

John Farr moved his lambs last night.
I open the back door onto their choir.
Water trickles down from the field
and the first warm day of the year
spins its soundtrack about the house –
mallards, wood pigeons, cockerels,
day-shift owls, tone-deaf crows,
all the hedgerow's penny whistles ...

Everything couples.
The sun settles on a silver ring.
The child I was draws a smile on my face.
Lambs bounce on their springs.
With a bale on its horn, a tractor
stops in the lane, to hear it sing.

Bridge 120

When it's time to slip back
inside the bricks, to disappear,
root into cracks, trail webs
on vaulted steel, let it be here.

Glazed with rain its crypt
already hears your ghost
when you call or stamp
on leaves, a girder's rust.

Desolate ecstasies fall,
lay Persian rugs
along the water's narrow hall.

The ivy's taken years
to reach down close enough
to touch, obsessively,
a friend's engraved love.

Here will do, for the echo,
for the mortar's florid vine
filtering through an arch
the incessant rain

a stone's insistence on glass

Not yet … Not yet …

All Souls Lay-by

Inside the hedge, a torn Union Jack and beyond, a scarecrow, waving back,
a tractor, ploughing the fields in our eyes.

We have lived and died in lay-bys,
queued for *Mari's Snax*, for a songbird, affected the heavy stillness of a herd,
its shuffle towards an imagined border.

A half-remembered picnic
slows the pulse. I think it was after rain – a rainbow leaking its oils, a breeze
that shook the dragon on its pole.

The beagle in the footwell snored, sedated.
The grandmother asked how many miles to go, to Babylon.

The father's
Hillman Minx sent up the age of steam from its overheated flask. Twin sisters
tricked their shadows. And genus dickie

pecked at the air's epiphanies,
the crumbs of love and laughter, murders, births, cardiac events ...

We have lived and died in lay-bys, bulls and heifers, mostly civil, taking care
not to tip the flies.

Mari stopped here *en route* to her wedding, and stayed.
It is half-way between two villages. One starry balalaika's night three spies
pulled in, exchanged burgers.

And one dark morning I came here to grieve,
inside a glass waterfall, for a son.

Let us half-pray, a plastic beaker
to our lips, sunlight under our chins, a cheddar cheese sandwich, wafer-thin

and before driving on, pick a shamrock for the bairns, a dandelion clock –
blow, seeds, blow – to tell the uncertain time by.

The Well of Song

I hardly know her younger voice.

The needle works towards
the hole time slips through.

Her lullaby, *Suo Gân*, slows,
falls flat, a candle guttering.

I place my hand over hers
as she placed hers over mine

and together we turn
till the flame rises again

and we are the same hand
at the windlass of song.

II
The Boys in the Branches

To His Sons

As suddenly as it arrives
a shower disappears.

This house keeps a silence
you would not believe.
To breathe is to haunt yourself!

Against a wall's glacier
a sunlit guitar
leans into its shadow.

Here's the mouser, old Syd,
loved like a Death Row cat.

A yellow acer in the window
colours in your absence.

Beyond it, three conifers
whirl to the wind's flamenco.

The Aeroplane

Jack, you tapped on my window
at the traffic lights in Bangalore,
near the temple of McDonald's.
You were eight or thereabouts,
trying to sell a toy aeroplane.

We clocked each other and smiled,
then struggled from both sides
to open the door's broken lock
as the taxi moved on, its driver
wearing my face in his mirror,
unable to hear our cries.

I looked back, as I must now,
waking again to see you there
on that wild runway,
a child clutching at sky.

The New Tenant

Your cot a tight fit in the white Fiat
which just fitted Audrey's drive.
Audrey, who called *Mum?... Dad?*
up the narrow stairs,
mistaking us for her parents.
She too was coming home.

Fireworks cracked the slate sky.
You slept through it all, each breath —
barely open, barely closed —
a tiny door to pause at, eavesdrop
on the stranger in the room.

Victoriana hemmed us in,
unfashionable darkness, shadows
in gilt frames, swags and bows
over the sink's dripping pulse

as the colours screamed all night
and Audrey called up
Mum?... Dad? in the early hours.
You slept through it all, Joe,
between a haunted tallboy
and Audrey's parents' bed

where we lay awake
as they must have, wide-eyed
at what love makes.

The Tree out the Back

Liz next door stalls her brush.
Don't look down, boys! Apples crash

back-heeled onto Mad Mal's shed.
He looks up, takes one on the head

as the boys climb and rusty leaves
cling on, and voices snap, and Liz

becomes her brush. You can't tell legs
from branches. A foot gets stuck.

And now the grizzly boughs bend
under the weight of three men.

Come down, boys! Now! Come down!
Mad Mal's bald, his mullet flown.

This minute! Please! Boys! Come down!
They carve their names on the late sun.

Ioan's Bridge

The mud river saws the town in two
as we cross in the floodlit mist.
A works hammer keeps time in its loom.

Still young enough to hold hands
you sing, without knowing,
a song with no beginning or end.

Our breath scales its rungs,
this song of a moment's mist.
And I am lost in its frail rigging

now that we have crossed.

Birthday Cut

The snip of steel in a shrunken garden.
This year his mother's on tip toes.

The sun comes and goes in her hand.
Last year's leaves play at her feet.

She blows on his neck, his shoulder blades.
The sun comes and goes in her hand.

In his ears, the breath of lullabies,
a silence that is understood.

She steps back and he gives a nod,
spying a man in the window's leaves.

Leaving 38

The boys kiss their bedroom doors
then, almost men, blink in the glare
at the top of the steps

                as if stage-struck
or woken from the middle of a dream,
or peering at the sun for the first time.

We brought them here in our arms.
The day is neither late summer
nor early autumn.

              The terrace hid us.
We kept to ourselves, our shadows
behind the tilted wooden blinds.

Our quiet song came and went.

There is never enough space to pack
the love that shapes itself to a house.

The removal van startles its engine.

A neighbour wishes us good luck.

At the Bridge

It is always the same –
the traffic lights on red

and the ghost boy at my side
whispering *Don't go*

as they turn to green.

Then a sense of flight

followed by a fall

as I cross without him.

Return to Newport

Our steep terrace drifts up to the moon.
A milkman bows to its doors.
Streetlights droop like Uri Geller spoons.
Strays hide knives in their paws.

A train scans its freight across the town
and into the tunnels of ears,
the tinnitus of a slowly breaking dawn.
This is how love disappears

under cover of dreams, tight-lipped blinds,
with the stealth of a milk thief.
And here is its patched roof, its flaking paint,
its laughter in the eaves.

The Winter Park

Ten years now, since I left
and the space between us widens
so we're ghostly when we meet
and yes, the heart hardens.

Our old life rarely haunts
but can still surprise.
This stone birdbath's font
for instance, suddenly ablaze

with a ritual. The boys sail twigs
in its brightness as you wait
on a bench for me, to come back
from the bookshop across the street –

your weekly gift, these minutes
alone, that pass into years,
a small park's blinding light,
and you not waiting here.

The Boys in the Branches

Perhaps they are hiding still,
beyond this trail's vaulted aisle

turning their bird-talk into words,
the rush of seasons in their ears.

I think I see their shadows
if I shield my eyes.

                    Don't cry.
They simply ran on ahead.

III
The Weight of the Sea

The Blood Tide

From the shallow-end of a day
wade out with me, Brown Helen.
We are not yet eleven
and the water's up to our knees.
No need to hold hands.
The sun brightens, the sprats are in
and stroking our feet.

Now it's noon and my voice breaks,
you've turned the sea red.
The years rise up to our waists.
The current levitates our steps
and the space between us widens.
You are drifting north to Cei Bach.
I am drifting south of the quay.

Already the sun arcs into the west,
its blood-and-thunder horizon.
We will have to trust in the tide,
in the light from *Penllain*'s porch
to bring us in, Brown Helen.
Two heads call to each other
across the wounded bay.

The Key to *Penllain*

'Through the floor my soul...'

Patrick Kavanagh – *Why Sorrow?*

I

All summer the key knows where it is
and all summer he searches
in pockets, plant-pots, drawers ...
in the sound-box of an old guitar.

And as the heatwave intensifies
in this summer of the lost key
he sprawls on the sofa

retraces the day it disappeared,
the laughter the key had opened,
the songs, the dusty light ...

The sky cracks. A claxon at sea.
Woods crack on the bowling green.
The hot rain loses the key again,
into a thousand drains.

Barefooted through the storm
he splashes to the hardware store,
returns with a hammer,
to break up the varnished floor.

All night raging on his knees
he finally lets go
as biblical lightning spies

a life's broken boatyard, a key
grinning at the earth's core,

his impatient shadow
at the door of a dream

trying a needle, a paper-clip,
a magnet, pliers, a pen-knife
and now a hair-grip ...

Neighbours gather.
The dead press their lips
to *Penllain*'s letter box,
whisper advice from a dark hall –

'For rings on fingers, try soap ...'

'Tongues in bottles, warm water ...'

'Gently now, we may not be here ...'

'Try ringing the bell!'

II

Inside the pause between
her answer, his walking away

the brush of summer doors
open and close
over vestibule floors.

He has not returned
for love but for the key
only Brown Helen can find

under a patch of sand
near the jetty.

A gull surfs the terrace
with a glint in its bill.

And the pity in her eyes,
the pity, when finally

Brown Helen appears.

III

She can spare an hour,
floats upstairs, to put on a year.
In Geta's sunken armchair
he waits in the back room

deep in the fathomless grate,
its bellows' pufferfish, kettle,
trident with the Bill Sykes handle.

The key is the secret key
each clock keeps behind its door
where the pendulum should be –

the start or the end of time,
or no time, he is not sure.
One clock says three, the other four.

A nest blocks the chimney.
A child's fishing net slips through glass.
Listen to it now, this aloneness

this darkness to build a fire inside,
the chime from the kitchen
as Geta's rice pudding goes in.

In the house of lost pendulums
the clocks are making up time,
Brown Helen has turned ten,
nurses a hot-mustard towel.

Let's go! And take your spade.
We'll dig for it.

He slides off the chair
into enormous sandals,
nine again, scared of her.

IV

I name this hour's rice pudding …
'Penllain'!

      The door slams
but the red rose in its glass
won't break because

               if it does
the hour seizes and they are not
winding

      steeply down to the sea
where it is most blinding
on Harbour Beach

            where the key
hides in the year of our sunburn
nineteen sixty-nine

somewhere below
the scattered human shoal.

V

Wading through fine sand
they pause by the trampolines
at the crowded sea wall –
his red spade, her yellow towel.

Helen, where do we dig?
She points to the lifeboat shed.

Red spade, yellow towel.
Pick them out …

side-stepping Hera
chained to her deckchair,
Hermes strumming some Dylan,
the midwife Elethea Gwyn ...

red spade, yellow towel

past Artemis and Apollo
arguing over a spear-gun,
over who was first to the moon ...

It was easy to lose, fool's silver,
a sprat's time-piece in the swell.
Yet one tick of the key's tail
turns the bay Aegean,

is an hour with Brown Helen.

Red spade, yellow towel

stepping over Hades' head,
hand-in-hand.

Here's where we dig.

VI

First the spade
then with bare hands.

*See how the sun lands
here, on this spot?*

The beach empties about them.
Its limes, ambers, scarlets,
tangos, orchid pinks, cyans ...

dissolve into Carnaby tan.

It has to be here!

A pleasure boat's megaphone
calls the last gods home.

In the harbour of lost pendulums
the masts are making up time.

Brown Helen is tired.
The sun reels in its lines.
The rice hour's tide comes in.

The brush of summer doors
open and close
over vestibule floors

and the spade snaps in its hole.

VII

A deep weight
hangs from their arms.

Both burrow now
with bare paws.

The harbour siren.
The darkening sky.

They lean over the rim
of childhood

and the key pulls them in
head first, arrow-heads
of the land and sea
that follow them
into the void
drinking
down

the snack bar,
trampolines, dinghies,
the stone pier

now Glanmor Terrace
and the houses behind
except *Penllain*

now the grazed acres
out to Cross Inn,
Llanarth, Ffos-y-ffin …

Into its last summer's
rabbit hole
the decade hauls

all years and eras,
the linear myth,

a plastic planet's
oceanic broth.

All creeds, empires,
famines, festivals

follow the key hunters
into the *O*

VIII

The ice-caps
have slipped their sticks.

A mezzo's *A*
below middle *C*

sustains the void.

Penllain, in a spin,
free from its terrace

floats in space

and now in silence –

the pause between

her answer

his walking away.

IX

Listen to this aloneness,
this darkness to build a fire inside.

Gingerly after her nap
Geta opens the oven door,
to check her *pwdin reis.*

She peers in, nods twice

and there is light.

X

First the laughter of children
in *Penllain*'s hall
then older, deeper tones

the sun again
through an art nouveau rose.

The hour has almost burnt
the skin on Geta's rice.

The clocks chime four and five
in the back room.

Helen holds up the key.

Geta raises her arms
in Alleluia disbelief.

Iesu Mawr! Where was it?

A child's fishing net
slips through glass.

XI

The parlour's splintered deck
comes into focus.
He has slept on his knees.

The sun hurts. A claxon at sea.
Woods crack on the bowling green.

All summer the key knows where it is
and all summer he searches.

Penllain at Sea

Penllain is crewless, on course for winter.
The grains of a hundred summers
stow away in its hold, its cellar,
its *twll dan grisiau*.

A pipe knocks in the engine room.

My cabin door slides open.
Tim Buckley's *Song to the Siren*
climbs the stairwell, enters a dream
of beds run aground in a storm.

I wake with icicles in my beard
and *swim to me... swim to me...*
in my ears

        the skylight angled
so I know she was here.

The Weight of the Sea

The weight of the sea between harbour walls
is the weight of this wanting you,
the weight of the sun and the moon.

Some days you are distant and still
as that sail on the horizon

but today your tide's in my veins
and these arms are the heavy stones
that went towards building the quay.

Cei Newydd

We drifted out one afternoon
on a dinghy's water-bed,

woke to no sight of the shore.
We had not been born.

A panic of oars
scratched the wilderness

and the harbour came back to us,
our mothers on the pier.

The salt on the fishing nets
tasted the same.

Soon, Brown Helen,
we shall drift out again.

Cân Hwyr

Dros afon gul mi glywais
y dail yn dilyn dy draed.

Clyw fi nawr, rhy hwyr –
llais y môr drwy'r coed

yn canu dy enw dros y dŵr.

Notes

Cat (pp. 11-14): *Catrin Sands* in previous collections.

Tauseef Akhtar (p.16): Renowned Ghazal singer and composer. *tauseefakhtar.com*

John the Clock (p.18): Horologist and cardiologist.

Picker Puw (p.23): Rev. D.J. Henry, Calvinistic Methodist Minister of Bwlch, Powys, 1945-1955.

Llŷr (p. 25): Welsh sea god. Circa 1970, Ted Pugh, the Cliff Railway driver in Aberystwyth, would each morning climb on his crutches the zig-zag, cliff-face path up Constitution Hill, to start the first train.

Admira and Boško (p.27): Admira Ismic and Boško Brkić, a young Bosniak and Serb couple, were killed by snipers on 18th May, 1993 as they tried to cross Sarajevo's Vrbanja Bridge. Their bodies lay embraced on the bridge for a week, until it was safe to recover them.

Penllain (pp. 51-61): A terraced house in Cei Newydd, Ceredigion.

Brown Helen (pp. 51-63): Sister of *Catrin Sands*, daughter of *Gwyneth Blue*.

Geta (pp. 54-60): Getta Thomas (1893-1982). Mamgu to *Brown Helen* and *Catrin Sands*. Late of *Penllain*. Famous, in her terrace, for her rice puddings.

Acknowledgements

Some of these poems first appeared in following publications:

Fallon's Angler, New Welsh Review, The North, Poetry Wales, The Spectator, The Times Literary Supplement.

'Dust o'clock' was commissioned by Swansea University for *The Strings of Song*, a celebratory response to the work of Vernon Watkins, held at Taliesin Arts Centre, Swansea.

'As if to Sing' was originally part of a longer poem, commissioned by *BBC Radio Wales* for Armistice Day 2018. The poem drew on Welsh veterans' accounts of the Battle of Passchendaele.

'Tributary' first appeared in the *Write Where We Are Now* web-pages: *mmu. ac.uk/write*

I am grateful to Stephen Knight and Jane Houston for their help with this collection's final stages. A Society of Authors 'Foundation Award' also helped with the book's completion.

My heartfelt thanks to Amy Wack who has edited my work for the past thirty years.

by the same author

Time Pieces
Captive Audience
The Milk Thief
The Slipped Leash
The Breath of Sleeping Boys & other poems
Ingrid's Husband
The Brittle Sea: New & Selected Poems
The Black Guitar: Selected Poems (India)
Boy Running
The Glass Aisle

Mari d'Ingrid (L'Harmattan, tr. Gérard Augustin)
Ragazzo di corsa (Kolibris, tr. Chiara De Luca)
Il corridoio di vetro (Kolibris, tr. Chiara De Luca)

The Slate Sea (Camden Trust, ed.)